Up the Rock

Written by Sarah Snashall

Illustrated by Nathalie Ortega

Collins

T0337215

We think this is fun.

rock

3

I check my kit.

Bang in a peg.

Zigzag up.

Fix in a cam.

Pull up quick.

We hang and chat ...

at the top!

Zip back.

I thank my chum.

/sh/

14

After reading

Letters and Sounds: Phase 3

Word count: 39

Focus phonemes: /ng/ /ch/ /nk/ /th/ /z/ /qu/ /x/

Common exception words: to, the, I, my, pull, we, and

Curriculum links: Physical Development; Personal, Social and Emotional Development

Early learning goals: Reading: read and understand simple sentences; use phonic knowledge to decode regular words and read them aloud accurately; read some common irregular words

Developing fluency

- Your child may enjoy hearing you read the book.
- Ask your child to read the sentences with expression, emphasising words for excitement, and pausing for suspense at the ellipsis on page 10.

Phonic practice

- On page 4, focus on the word **check**. Ask your child to find the pairs of letters that each make one sound. (*/ch/ and /ck/*)
- Ask your child to find the two letters that make one sound in each of these words: **rock**, **link**, **bang**, **pull**, **hang**, **back**, **chum**.
- Look at the "I spy sounds" pages (14–15). Point to the ship and say "ship", emphasising the /sh/ sound. Point to the chickens and say "chickens", emphasising the /ch/ sound. Challenge your child to find more words containing these sounds. Explain that the sound can be at the beginning or end of the words, too. (*e.g. sheep, shed, shoes, shells, shovel, chair, bench, chips, chilli, beach*)

Extending vocabulary

- Point to **zigzag** on page 7. Ask your child what else can move in a zigzag way, or is shaped like a zigzag? (*e.g. snake, road markings, pattern on a jumper, mountain path, stitching*)
- Read the text on page 9. Ask your child if they can think of the opposite of **pull** (*push*) and the opposite of **quick** (*slow*).
- Read page 12 and ask your child if they can think of words that could be used instead of **zip**. (*e.g. whizz, zoom*)